MEATLESS MEALS FOR WORKING PEOPLE

QUICK AND EASY VEGETARIAN RECIPES

Recipes tested and developed on the Appalachian Trail, the Delaware Shore, at food demonstrations in Maryland, and hotel rooms of Rhode Island, among other places which necessitated quick and easy dishes.

Copyright © 1986, 1990, updated 1991 by Debra Wasserman and Charles Stahler. Fast food information updated in 1996 by Michael Keevican.

ISBN 0-931411-06-8

10 9 8 7 6

The
VEGETARIAN
Resource Group

Table of Contents

Eggless Banana Pancakes 23; Pepper/Onion/Egg Scramble 23; Hash Brown Potatoes 23; Cinnamon/Sliced Apple Toast 24; Cornbread And Blueberries 24; Applesauce 24; Eggless French Toast 25; Oatmeal/Apples/Raisins And Cinnamon 25; Corn Meal Mush 25

Hot Apple Cider 26; Blended Fruit Drink 26; Quick Cashew Milk 26; Easy Almond Milk 27; "Milk" Shake 27; Sparkling Seltzer 27

Coleslaw 28; A Hefty Salad 28; Stuffed Tomato Salad 28; Cucumber Salad 29; Beet Salad 29; Summer Fruit Salad 29; Potato Salad And Olives 30; Macaroni Salad 30; Tomato Salad 31; Cranberry Salad 31; Sweet Rainbow Delight 31; Raw Vegetable Platter 32; Sweet French Dressing 32; Lemon/Apple/Garlic Dressing 32; Red Beet Dressing 32

VEGETARIANISM IN A NUTSHELL

Vegetarianism is the abstinence from meat, fish or fowl. Among the many reasons for being a vegetarian are compassion for animals, aesthetic considerations, ecological, economic, spiritual, and health reasons. The American Dietetic Association has affirmed that a vegetarian diet can meet all known nutrient needs. LIKE EVERY DIET, THE KEY TO A HEALTHY VEGETARIAN DIET IS SIMPLE. Eat a variety of foods, eat a lot of greens, and have high-fat, high-salt, empty-calorie foods as only a small part of your diet. For the minority, but growing number, of vegetarians who abstain from milk and eggs (vegans) this also can be done easily, but you may want to talk to others who have been practicing this diet.

Our gratitude and thanks to:

Ruth Ransom R.D., Suzanne Havala R.D., Ruth Stahler, Susan Meyers, Sherman Pratt, Chris Stadler, Cindy Blum, Audrey Fluke, Tina Blatter, Sally Clinton, Ernie Kopstein M.D., Mort Randolph, Norris Fluke, Stephen Havala, and Emma Pride Wood.

A special thanks to Gayle Miller who supplied us with many of the drawings appearing in this book.

Fresh is Best, But . . .

Using frozen, canned and prepackaged foods greatly decreases food preparation time whether you are on a vegetarian diet or eating meat foods. Beware, however, that many prepackaged foods are high in sodium and may have animal shortening in them.

FROZEN FOODS

Frozen foods can be stored easily, and quickly popped into the oven while you're changing your clothes after work. Frozen vegetables such as green beans, corn, and spinach can be cooked in a short time and eaten by themselves or combined with other ingredients. Beware not to overcook or use too much water. Green Giant and other companies have many variations of vegetables with butter and cheese sauces. Legume offers frozen tofu entrees which can be served for lunch or dinner.

CANNED AND PREPACKAGED VEGETARIAN FOODS

Though often more expensive than preparing from scratch, there are numerous canned and prepackaged foods you can find in most supermarkets that can quickly be used to have a snack or prepare a meal.

DAIRY CASE

Your dairy case is packed full of vegetarian ingredients and fast meal possibilities. Try to select low-fat dairy products.

Suggested Vegetarian Meals

These are quick dishes that you probably know how to cook already and can be made from common supermarket foods. For a main meal, you may have one large central dish, a sandwich, or many side dishes.

SANDWICHES:

Hunts Manwich Sloppy Joe Sauce and vegetables
Peanut butter and jelly
Cream cheese and jelly
Cheese, lettuce and tomato
Bagels and margarine or cream cheese
Egg salad
Grilled cheese
Peanut butter and sliced bananas
Baked beans and lettuce on toast

MAIN MEALS (lunch or dinner):

Macaroni and cheese (frozen or boxed)
Spaghetti and cheese or sauce (canned)
Cheese lasagna (frozen)
Other pasta (rigatoni, twists, etc.)
Blintzes (potato, cheese, etc.)
Pierogis
Cheese pizza (frozen or from the dairy case)
Yogurt and fruit
Cottage cheese
Bean taco (dairy case, boxed kit or frozen)
Tortillas and burritos (boxed kit or dairy case)
Soups (Progresso has delicious thick soups)

Manicotti (frozen)
Eggplant Parmesan (frozen)
Chinese food (packaged, frozen or canned such as fried
rice with almonds)
Instant biscuit mix combined with vegetables and
water to make a quick, filling, thick soup

SIDE DISHES:

Stuffing mix (eg. Stove Top)
Canned vegetables (beets, lima beans, butter beans,
kidney beans, vegetarian baked beans, spinach, peas,
mixed beans, corn, etc.)
Frozen vegetables
Instant mashed potatoes
Salads at deli counter or salad bar
Hash browns (frozen)
Tater Tots (frozen)
Onion rings (frozen)
Rice-A-Roni (can easily be made into a main dish by
adding chopped vegetables, etc.)
Instant rice
Three bean salad (can be a main dish also)
Soups (tomato, cream of mushroom, noodle, cream of
asparagus, etc. You can buy these in cans, boxed or
frozen)

CONDIMENTS:

Tomato sauce
Mustard
Pickles
Olives
Sauerkraut
Juices
Chow mein noodles
Relish

BREADS:

English muffins
Bagels
Rye bread
White bread (if you must)
Italian bread
French bread
Raisin bread
Garlic bread (often available in freezer case)
Hard rolls
Kaiser rolls
Whole wheat bread
Pita bread

BREAKFASTS:

These can easily be served as main meals. Try to limit your use of eggs.

Frozen waffles
Frozen French toast
Pancake/waffle mix
Oatmeal, grits, etc.
Cream of wheat
Dry cereals (Nutri-grain, Shredded Wheat, Puffed Rice, etc.)
Breakfast strips, soy sausages, such as Morningstar (beware, these are often high in sodium)
Eggs any style (scrambled, boiled, fried, etc.)
Omelettes (plain or add vegetables and cheese)
Egg beaters
Cornbread
Fruit
Toast and margarine
Leftovers from dinner

DESSERTS AND SNACKS:

Applesauce
Ice cream or soy ice cream (Tofutti, Ice Bean, etc.)
Ices
Sherbet
Raisins
Nuts and seeds
Popcorn
Dried fruit
Crackers
Fruit salad
Baked apples and pears (you can core them and add
    cinnamon and dates)
Soft pretzels
Frozen juices (you can put a popsicle stick in while
    freezing)
Bread sticks and dips or spreads

TAKE OUT FOODS:

The quickest way to prepare a meal is to take out food.
Stop at your local deli counter and pick up potato salad,
health salads, and other goodies. Ethnic fast food
places are also good resources. You can get bean tacos
or burritos, vegetable lo mein and/or stir fried vegetables. Most Chinese restaurants will make any dish that
has meat or fish in it with just vegetables if you politely
ask. Pizza and eggplant subs are also great take out
items. Often restaurants fry their food in lard, so you
may want to ask some questions before ordering.

Eating Out

Eating out is getting easier and easier for vegetarians. If you have a choice, try an ethnic restaurant. Besides Chinese, Mexican, and Italian, good vegetarian eateries in larger cities are Indian, Middle Eastern, and Ethiopian. And, of course, even fast food places and truck stops now have salad bars. (See our list of vegetarian offerings in fast food restaurants in this book.)

TRUCK STOPS AND SHOPPING CENTERS:

Following are vegetarian items we've found in these places.

Salad bars
Eggs
Grits
Hash browns
Waffles
Pancakes
Salads
Vegetable soup
French fries
Lettuce and tomato sandwiches with cheese
Grilled cheese sandwiches
Coleslaw
Eggplant Parmesan
Pretzels
Ice cream
Nuts and seeds
Fruit
Yogurt
Vegetables (side orders)
English muffins, bagels, etc.
Onion rings

BOARDWALKS, CARNIVALS AND PARKS:

Even these havens of typical Americana have plenty of alternatives for the vegetarian.

Ice cream
French fries
Pizza
Fruit cups
Pretzels with mustard
Onion rings
Milk or fruit shakes
Funnel cakes
Fried dough
Corn on the cob
French fried vegetables
Cheese subs (hoagie, grinder, etc.)
Popcorn

Vegetarians certainly aren't in danger of starving. Even airlines will offer vegetarian meals. The one time we would suggest you be sure to carry your own food is if you have to go to the hospital!

VEGETARIAN FOOD ON AIRLINES:

If you require a special meal for reasons of health, religion, or personal preference, most airlines will accommodate your needs if you let them know 24 hours before departure. We would recommend that you tell your food requirements to the airline when making your reservation and then remind them again 24 hours before your flight is due to depart.

Special meals available may include bland-soft, diabetic, Kosher, vegetarian with dairy, vegetarian without dairy or eggs (vegan), and low-cholesterol. Be specific about what you are requesting. Beware that the low-cholesterol meal probably contains an animal product. Most airlines will serve you a tv dinner, but the vegetarian meal is still often better than what others receive.

Fast Food

Where can I go to eat out? Many strict vegetarians stay away from restaurants where there is the slightest possibility their food may be "contaminated." Others hesitatingly join with their friends for a quick bite, either picking at the food or bringing their own salad dressing, sandwich, etc. Animal rights activists have organized boycotts against Burger King for selling veal and Icelandic fish. (Iceland was a target because its fishermen harmed marine mammals.) Burger King responded positively to the animal rights protests. There was also a protest against McDonald's and now they serve salads. McDonald's has also been test marketing packaged carrot and celery sticks in some stores.

Should we give our money to these places? Each individual must make his or her own choice. If a fast food chain earns a profit from selling vegetarian food, it will offer more vegetarian items. If there is no market, the choice will not be available. Others would say we should not, from an ethical perspective, encourage dining in fast food restaurants because doing so supports destruction of the world environment and affects family unity by lessening the time for dining together at home. On the other hand, some families enjoy eating out together at these restaurants. What do you think?

WHAT'S IN FAST FOOD?

Following is information that fast food chains sent to us. Though we mailed letters to over 100 businesses, not all answered us when updating this section in 1994. In the past, the lack of knowledge about ingredients in their food has astounded us, but at present it seems that some improvements are being made in this area. We do thank those companies that did respond.

CAUTION: When you eat out, you can never be 100% certain that food is vegetarian. Ask at the restaurant. Often policy and ingredients change. Different restaurants in the same chain may use different ingredients to produce the same item. Even when you inquire, the people working there may not know, or because of lack of knowledge, may give you incorrect information. The facts that follow were taken from letters supplied by the parent companies. Though most readers will only care if the food is vegetarian (contains no meat, fish, or fowl), in some cases we also gave information for *vegans* concerning animal by-products such as milk, eggs, whey and other animal derivatives.

ARBY'S: Arby's is now using vegetable oil for its fried foods. Their buns contain eggs or milk derivatives. Arby's offers the Garden Salad, which contains cheese, and a vegan small side salad. They also offer a baked potato, and they are presently testing vegetable pita pockets which contain broccoli, carrots, cauliflower, and celery. The milkshakes and the cheese contain animal rennet (as most cheese does).

BASKIN ROBBINS: Most Baskin Robbins' desserts are vegetarian and some are even vegan. Flavors made with marshmallow, however, contain animal gelatin. Dairy-free products include Ices and Sorbet. Most of their products are also egg-free with the exception of Egg Nog, French Vanilla, Vanilla, and Custard flavors, and those with cookie or cake pieces.

BOB'S BIG BOY: Bob's Big Boy, part of Marriott Corporation's family restaurant division, contains a decent selection for vegetarians, though options for vegans are limited. For breakfast there are cereal, potatoes, pancakes, French toast, bagels, toast, muffins, and a wide selection of fresh fruit.

Another pleasant surprise at Bob's is a Garden Lasagna, which is a vegetarian lasagna containing cheese, spinach, carrots, and onions.

BONANZA: Their restaurants are individually franchised. Because menu items vary among regions and are purchased from a wide listing of manufacturers and distributors, any nutritional evaluation done on one unit's products would be invalid for the rest. Vegetable items, salads and desserts on their salad bars are purchased locally. Ask managers for details.

BURGER KING: Burger King uses only vegetable oil for their fried products. Animal products such as chicken or fish are fried in separate deep frying vats than those used for fries, onion rings, or hash browns.

Other vegetarian options at Burger King include the garden and side salads, croissants, bagels, blueberry muffins, and lemon pie. The cherry and apple pies contain casein (a milk derivative), and the Snickers Ice Cream Bar contains gelatin.

Burger King actually has a Veggie Whopper, which is cheese on a bun with whatever condiments and toppings you would like. They will also make it without cheese. Beware that the Whopper buns may contain animal shortening, but the hamburger buns are purchased locally; so ask when you go in. Their bagels are made with vegetable shortening, but contain egg whites. Onion rings contain whey, but their hash browns and French fries appear to be vegan. Burger King probably has the best quality salad dressings of the fast food chains, since they use Paul Newman's dressings, which avoid using preservatives and artificial ingredients. Burger King's Reduced Calorie Italian, French, and Oil & Vinegar dressings appear to be vegan. Their garden salad contains cheese. The side salad lists only lettuce, tomatoes, cucumber, celery, and radishes.

CARL'S JR.: Their French fries, onion rings, zucchini and other fried foods are cooked in vegetable oil. Their onion rings and zucchini contain dairy derivatives. Bread products which contain no animal shortening, eggs, or dairy derivatives include the breadsticks, hot dog bun, plain bun, flour tortilla, English muffin, and kaiser bun. None of their baked goods contain animal shortening. They have an all-you-can-eat salad bar, as well as macaroni, potato, and pasta salads in some stores. They also offer a Lite Potato with margarine on the side. Carl's Jr. is making efforts to remove MSG from all their menu items.

CHI-CHI'S: Chi-Chi's restaurants uses soybean oil to prepare their refried beans and other deep-fried items. They list the following items as being vegetarian: Chips and Salsa (vegan), Vegetable Chajita (vegan), Cheese Nachos, Guacamole, Chili Con Queso, Vegetable and Spinach Quesadillas, Cheese and Onion Enchiladas, Mexican Fried Ice Cream, and Mexican Salad. However, most of their cheeses do contain rennet, which is an enzyme from the stomach of calves. You can request their pepperjack cheese, which we were told does not contain animal rennet. Although they are using vegetable oil for all of their fried foods, meat products are fried in the same oil as vegetarian products.

CHURCH'S FRIED CHICKEN: Vegetarian options at Church's include coleslaw, French fries, okra, and mashed potatoes without gravy. They said that they fry their okra in all vegetable shortening, but it is the same oil in which they fry their chicken nuggets.

DAIRY QUEEN: Dairy Queen/Brazier stores use only vegetable shortening to prepare their foods, and the only food they fry is French fries. Ingredients in buns and onion rings depend upon the local supplier. They offer a Garden Salad, which contains eggs, and a side salad which is apparently vegan.

DEL TACO: Bean burritos, quesadillas, and tostadas are all vegetarian and if the cheese is left out, they are vegan. Refried beans are prepared with 100% soybean oil and all sauces are meat-free.

DENNY'S: Denny's has a variety of choices for each meal. For breakfast, buttermilk biscuits, hash browns, French toast, and waffles are available, along with seasonal fruits. For dinner and lunch there are also a few choices. A garden salad is offered with eggs as a garnish, but they can be omitted. There is a variety of side dishes, including French fries and onion rings, both of which appear to be vegan, as well as mozzarella sticks, and cream of broccoli soup, which contains dairy but does not have an animal base. All their foods are prepared in vegetable oil, but vegetarian items are cooked in the same oil as meat products. There are two vegetarian sandwiches available -- grilled cheese and a veggie cheese melt. Breads are purchased locally and may contain dairy derivatives, and many of their cheeses contain animal rennet.

DOMINO'S: There are four different ingredient groupings for Domino's pizza crust, and any one of these might be used in your local units. Only one of these recipes is apparently vegan. The rest contain whey, and may contain egg, butter, buttermilk, cheese, and other dairy derivatives. None of these recipes contains lard. Their sauce appears to be vegan. The enzymes in their cheese is listed as being either of vegetable or animal origin.

EL CHICO'S: They use only vegetable oil for frying. Their refried beans reportedly do not contain lard, but you may want to check at your local restaurant.

EL POLLO LOCO Items available include a vegetarian burrito, corn, potato salad, coleslaw, and a salad.

HARDEE'S: Hardee's uses vegetable oil to cook all fried products. They offer pre-made salads including a garden salad which contains cheese and a side salad which is vegan. Other vegetarian possibilities at Hardee's include pancakes, hash rounds, egg and cheese biscuit, coleslaw, mashed potatoes, yogurt, and fries. Hardee's biscuits contain buttermilk and their gravy is sausage-based. Their Crispy Curls and French fries are fried separately from their fried meat products. Hardee's will make a cheese sandwich with toppings, but the cheese contains animal rennet.

JACK IN THE BOX: They cook with a griddle shortening that is a 100% vegetable oil blend, but the ingredients for this blend include natural butter flavor. The shortening blend for the fryers contains no animal products. As a rule they fry French fries and onion rings separately from the meats, but this is not strictly enforced. Bread products which appear to be vegan include their English muffins, hamburger bun, sesame breadsticks, tortilla bowl (wheat), pita bread, and gyro bread. The croissants contain nonfat dry milk and butter, and the sourdough bread is grilled with shortening. The onion rings contain whey and egg yolk solids. Hash browns and guacamole appear to be vegan. The seasoned curly fries contain nonfat dry milk. Jack in the Box offers a side salad which is vegan. The reduced calorie French dressing contains nonfat yogurt, but the low-calorie Italian dressing appears to be vegan with the possible exception of the "natural ingredients." Their "secret sauce" contains egg yolks and Worcestershire sauce (anchovies). The cinnamon churritos contain dairy products and the cheesecake contains gelatin, but the apple turnover is vegan.

KENTUCKY FRIED CHICKEN: KFC, as they prefer to be called these days, uses only vegetable shortening in all of its frying procedures, but their potato wedges are fried in the same oil as the chicken. Their bread products contain egg products. Some stores carry a garden salad which is vegan. Other options include corn on the cob, coleslaw, fries, plain buttermilk biscuits, mashed potatoes, which contain butter and milk, Italian pasta salad, macaroni and cheese, and vegetable medley. The garden rice, green beans, mean greens, red beans and rice, and BBQ baked beans all contain meat or meat flavorings. Side dishes differ from store to store.

LITTLE CAESARS: Little Caesars claims that currently, most use microbial or vegetable rennet in their cheese, but the Dallas, Greensboro, Atlanta, and Chicago area use calf rennet; so your best bet is to ask at each location. Their dough and tomato sauce are vegan. You can order Little Caesars pizza without cheese. Other options for vegetarians include a Veggie Sandwich, Greek Salad (contains feta cheese), Tossed Salad, Crazy Bread, and Crazy Sauce. Items that are vegan are the Crazy Sauce, Crazy Bread without Parmesan cheese, Tossed Salad, and Greek Salad ordered without feta cheese.

LONG JOHN SILVER'S: Their fried foods are prepared in partially hydrogenated soybean oil. The fries and hush puppies are prepared in the same oil as the meats. They offer prepared salads, corn on the cob, and green beans.

McDONALD'S: Fries and hash browns are both cooked in 100% vegetable oil in the USA, and are supposed to be fried in separate vats than those used for meat. However, in Canada and some other countries the fries are pre-cooked with beef tallow. They offer a garden salad which includes eggs, and a side salad which is vegan. Beware that their Red French Reduced Calorie dressing lists Worcestershire sauce which contains anchovies. Their only dressing that appears to be vegan is the Lite Vinaigrette. For breakfast, vegetarian options include hash browns, apple bran or English muffins, and cereal. All the Danish contain gelatin. McDonaldland cookies and apple pie appear to be vegan; the lecithin used is soy derived.

NATHAN'S: Their thick French fries are cooked in corn oil. Corn on the cob is often available.

PIZZA HUT: Their Pan Crust contains whey, but the Thin'n Crispy Crust and Hand-Tossed crusts are vegan. The breadsticks contain whey. Their pizza sauce contains MSG and cheese flavor, which is made with animal enzymes. A meat base is used in the pasta sauce. The cheese on pizzas contains synthetic rennet.

RAX: Rax is now using only Crisco, an all vegetable shortening, for their fried foods. However, their beans are first cooked with lard. Their crackers and croutons may contain animal shortening and their buns contain milk powder. Some of their pasta is vegan, but the rainbow rotini contains egg whites. Their sauce contains Parmesan cheese. Rax has a salad bar.

ROUND TABLE PIZZA: The cheese used on their pizza does not contain animal rennet. They have a good variety of vegetable toppings. Their dough and tomato sauce are vegan.

SHAKEY'S: Shakey's uses vegetable oil for frying, and all of their dough contains vegetable shortening. We were unable to determine whether or not their dough contained dairy products or if their cheese contains animal rennet. They have a salad bar.

SKIPPER'S: Skipper's uses soybean oil for frying all of their menu items. Their bread and breadsticks contain dairy products, but their crackers do not contain any animal products. They offer a garden salad which includes mixed greens, cucumbers, tomatoes, and carrots. Other vegetarian foods include baked potatoes, zucchini slices, and coleslaw made with mayonnaise. They also have onion rings which are made with a beer-based batter that is vegan.

TACO BELL: Taco Bell had added a new line of lowfat dishes; however, as we go to press they are eliminating the lowfat options and reformulating their products. In the past on the original menu both the corn tortillas (hard tacos) and wheat tortillas (soft tacos) were vegan. The heat pressed flour tortillas used for burritos do contain non-fat dry milk. On the lowfat menu the corn and wheat tortillas were vegan, as well as the light heat pressed tortillas used for the lowfat burritos. Corn or soy oil is used in all frying processes. The beans are vegan. Cheeses in the dishes may contain animal rennet or vegetable enzymes; this differs from store to store. Taco Bell's guacamole contains sour cream. For dessert the Cinnamon Twists and Border Ice products are vegan.

TACOTIME: TacoTime uses vegetable oil for their deep friers. Their refritos are made with vegetable shortening. Tortillas are vegan. Vegetarian dishes available at TacoTime include: soft bean burrito, crisp bean burrito, refritos (bean, sauce, and cheese), tostado, nachos, and Mexi-Fries.

WENDY'S: Wendy's SuperBar has one of the best salad bars in the fast food arena. They have removed the "natural beef flavor" from the spaghetti sauce, making it vegan. This can be served over vegan rotini. At the Mexican Fiesta, the refried beans no longer contain lard. Their Spanish rice contains natural flavorings, which may be animal derived. Their taco chips, taco sauce, and taco shells appear to be vegan. The flour tortillas contain whey. The deluxe garden salad and the side salad are both vegetarian, but do list imitation cheese as an ingredient. You can make a salad at the Garden Spot salad bar. Vegan dressings include French, Sweet Red French, Golden Italian, and Reduced Calorie Italian. The croutons contain whey, but the chow mein noodles appear to be vegan.

Recipes

The toughest barriers to quick and easy vegetarian cooking are the habits we have developed throughout our lifetime. Once you break that mental resistance, ideas for meals will come to you naturally, meal preparation will become routine and go much faster. This section has some ideas to get you started. You may want to adjust the amount of spices to your taste. Eliminate salt and soy sauce/tamari if you're on a low-salt diet. Use soy milk or nut milk instead of cow's milk and soy margarine instead of butter if you are trying to avoid animal products. Also, if you are on a restricted diet, when a recipe calls for oil for sauteing vegetables, use slightly more water instead of the oil.

Breakfast Ideas

EGGLESS BANANA PANCAKES (Serves 2)

1/2 Cup rolled oats
1/2 Cup flour
1/2 Cup corn meal (white or yellow)
1 Tablespoon baking powder
1 1/2 Cups water
2-3 bananas, sliced or mashed

Mix all the ingredients together in a bowl. Pour batter into oiled pre-heated frying pan. Fry over low heat on one side until done, then flip over and fry on the other side.

Variations: Add apples, raisins, or blueberries.

PEPPER/ONION/TOFU SCRAMBLE
(Serves 2-3)

2 Tablespoons oil
1 green pepper, chopped finely
1 small onion, chopped
1 pound soft tofu crumbled

Saute onion and pepper in oil for 3 minutes. Add tofu to mixture in frying pan. Stir-fry 5 minutes longer and serve warm.

HASH BROWN POTATOES (Serves 4)

4 large potatoes, cleaned and sliced
1 large onion, chopped

Heat some oil in a frying pan. Add potatoes and onion. Season with garlic powder, paprika, pepper and salt. Stir and fry until potatoes are soft.

CINNAMON/SLICED APPLE TOAST
(Serves 6)

2-3 apples, sliced
1 Tablespoon brown sugar (optional)
1 Tablespoon margarine
1/2 teaspoon cinnamon
whole wheat bread or English muffins

Toast bread. Place a slice of apple, dots of margarine, sprinkle of brown sugar and a dash of cinnamon on toast. Place under broiler until the margarine melts.

CORNBREAD AND BLUEBERRIES (Serves 6)

1 box cornbread mix (Beware: many mixes contain lard!)
1 Cup blueberries (or other fruit)

Add blueberries to batter prepared from cornbread mix. Pour into oiled cake pan. Bake until done at 350 degrees (approximately 15 minutes).

APPLESAUCE (Serves 6)

6 apples, diced finely
1 Tablespoon cinnamon
1 teaspoon nutmeg
2 oranges, peeled and sliced
water

Fill bottom of large pot with water and cook above ingredients over medium heat until the apples are soft.

Variation: Add raisins.

EGGLESS FRENCH TOAST (Serves 3-4)

3 ripe bananas
1 Cup milk
2 Tablespoons molasses or maple syrup
1/4 teaspoon cinnamon
7 slices whole wheat bread

Mash bananas in a bowl. Add milk, molasses or maple syrup, and cinnamon. Stir well.

Soak bread in above mixture. Fry in margarine or oil on both sides over medium heat.

OATMEAL/APPLES/RAISINS AND CINNAMON (Serves 4)

1 Cup rolled oats
3 Cups water
2 apples, chopped
1/2 Cup raisins
1 teaspoon cinnamon

Heat the above ingredients together in a pot over a medium heat until oats are cooked.

Variation: Use quick oats instead of rolled oats and follow cooking directions on the box.

CORN MEAL MUSH (Serves 2)

1/2 Cup quick cooking corn meal
1 1/2 Cups water
1/2 Cup chopped fresh fruit (blueberries, bananas, strawberries, etc.)

Cook corn meal in water according to directions on the box, adding chopped fruit just before serving.

Beverages

HOT APPLE CIDER (Serves 8)

1/2 gallon apple cider
1 lemon, sliced thinly
1 or 2 teaspoons cinnamon
1/4 teaspoon nutmeg

Heat above ingredients in a large pot over a medium heat, stirring occasionally, until heated through.

BLENDED FRUIT DRINK (Serves 4)

3 ripe bananas
6 strawberries
4 Cups orange juice

Blend and serve cold.

Variations: Use different fruit juices and other fruits such as peaches and apples.

QUICK CASHEW MILK (Serves 4)

1 Cup raw cashews
3 Cups water

Blend both ingredients together for 5 minutes and re-frigerate. Use as beverage or in recipes calling for milk. Shake well before serving.

EASY ALMOND NUT MILK (Serves 2)

1/2 Cup almonds
1 1/2 Cups boiling water

Blend almonds and boiling water together for about 3 minutes at a high speed. Strain through muslin or cheesecloth. The remaining pulp can be used in vegetable/nut loaves or burgers. Shake milk well before serving.

"MILK" SHAKE (Serves 3)

3 Cups nut milk (see above recipes)
6 Tablespoons cocoa or carob powder
2/3 Cup shredded coconut
sweetener to taste (maple syrup, etc.)

Blend above ingredients together at a high speed for 2 minutes. Serve chilled.

SPARKLING SELTZER (Serves 1)

8 ounces seltzer (salt free)
2 Tablespoons frozen juice concentrate (orange, grape, lemon, grapefruit, etc.)

Pour chilled seltzer into a glass. Add frozen juice concentrate. Stir well and serve.

Variation: Add 1/2 Cup juice instead of frozen concentrate to 1/2 Cup of seltzer. Stir and serve.

Salads And Dressings

COLESLAW (Serves 4)

1/2 head cabbage, shredded
4 carrots, grated
1/2 Cup lemon juice
1/2 Cup mayonnaise

Mix all ingredients together in a large bowl.

Variations: Add grated apples, crushed pineapple, raisins and/or sunflower seeds.

A HEFTY SALAD (Serves 4)

1 stalk celery, diced
1 large carrot, grated
1 clove garlic, minced (optional)
1/2 Cup toasted sunflower seeds
2 Tablespoons mayonnaise or dressing of choice
salt and pepper to taste

Mix well and serve on lettuce or raw spinach leaves. Sprinkle with grated Parmesan cheese.

STUFFED TOMATO SALAD (Serves 5)

5 large ripe tomatoes
1 can garbanzo beans (or 1 Cup precooked chickpeas or
   garbanzo beans)
1 stalk celery, chopped (optional)
salt and pepper to taste

Scoop out tomatoes, saving pulp for a sauce. Fill tomatoes with beans and celery. Season with salt and pepper. Garnish with sauce and lettuce or sprouts.

CUCUMBER SALAD (Serves 6)

3 cucumbers, sliced
1/2 Cup vinegar
1 small onion, minced
pepper to taste

Mix ingredients together. This can be served immediately; however, it tastes better if allowed to sit in the refrigerator for a day or two. Store in a jar.

BEET SALAD (Serves 4)

2 beets, grated
1/2 head of cabbage, shredded
3 carrots, grated
handful of raisins
1 apple, diced
1/4 Cup lemon juice
1/2 Cup oil

Toss ingredients into bowl and mix well.

Variations: Use raw sweet potato instead of beets. Add sunflower seeds, crushed pineapple or other fruit.

SUMMER FRUIT SALAD (Serves 12)

fresh pineapple
fruit in season

Stand pineapple upright and cut in half vertically. Carve out pineapple into bite size pieces. Cut up additional fruits into small pieces. Mix fruit together and pour back into pineapple shell. Sprinkle with shredded coconut and serve chilled.

POTATO SALAD AND OLIVES (Serves 4)

4 large potatoes, cubed into very small pieces
water
1 box frozen, mixed vegetables
1 onion, chopped finely
1/2 can black olives, drained and sliced
mayonnaise
1 teaspoon celery seed
salt and pepper to taste

Cover potatoes with water and cook. At the same time, cook vegetables in a separate pot. Mix all ingredients together in a large bowl. Season and add mayonnaise according to your taste.

Variations: Instead of frozen vegetables, add raw vegetables such as celery and carrots. Add parsley. You may want to use canned Irish potatoes to save time.

MACARONI SALAD (Serves 6)

2 Cups macaroni, cooked
2 stalks celery, diced
1 carrot, diced
1 Cup peas (frozen or fresh)
1 small onion, chopped finely
mayonnaise
salt and pepper to taste

Cook macaroni. Cook peas. Mix all the ingredients in a large bowl. Season and add mayonnaise.

Variations: Add sliced pickles, other vegetables, or olives.

TOMATO SALAD (Serves 4)

4 tomatoes, cut in 1/2 inch wedges
1/3 Cup oil
1 teaspoon lemon juice
2 cloves of garlic, minced
oregano and salt to taste

Mix all ingredients together in a bowl and serve.

CRANBERRY SALAD (Serves 12)

Blend together:
12 ounces fresh or frozen cranberries
1/2 Cup orange juice or apple juice
1 Cup raisins

Add in a bowl and mix:
1 Cup shredded coconut
2 stalks celery, chopped finely
1 apple, chopped finely

Optional: Add chopped walnuts.

SWEET RAINBOW DELIGHT (Serves 6)

2 apples, grated
2 carrots, grated
2/3 Cup shredded coconut
1/2 Cup raisins
1/2 Cup chopped walnuts

Toss all ingredients together in a bowl and serve.

Variation: Add chopped dates instead of raisins.

RAW VEGETABLE PLATTER (Serves 12)

Chop up into bite size pieces 3-4 pounds of vegetables including: celery, carrots, broccoli, tomatoes, squash, and mushrooms. Arrange on a large platter. Serve with your favorite dips and spreads or the dressings below.

SWEET FRENCH DRESSING (Makes 2 Cups)

1 Cup oil
2 oranges, peeled and seeds taken out
2 Tablespoons lemon juice
1 Tablespoon vinegar
1 teaspoon each salt and paprika
slice of onion, minced

Blend all the ingredients together for 3 minutes.

LEMON/APPLE/GARLIC DRESSING
(Makes 3 Cups)

1 Cup vinegar
1 1/2 Cups water
2 Tablespoons lemon juice
2 cloves garlic, minced
1/4 teaspoon each pepper and salt
1 apple, chopped

Blend all the ingredients together for 3 minutes.

RED BEET DRESSING (Makes 2 Cups)

Blend the following together for 3 minutes:
1 beet, peeled and chopped
1 Cup orange juice
1/2 Cup oil
1 clove garlic, minced
Salt and pepper to taste

Soups

VEGETABLE BARLEY SOUP (Serves 6-8)

1 Cup barley
6 Cups water
1/2 Cup parsley, chopped
2 Cups frozen mixed vegetables
1 onion, chopped
pepper and salt to taste

Cook all the ingredients in a large pot over medium heat until barley is tender.

FRESH TOMATO SOUP (Serves 4)

1 large onion, chopped
5 small ripe tomatoes, chopped
1 1/2 Cups water
1 teaspoon parsley flakes or equivalent fresh
dash of pepper and salt

Combine ingredients in a large pot. Cook over medium heat for 15 minutes. Cool a few minutes. Then blend in a blender, reheat, and serve.

CARROT CREAM SOUP (Serves 6)

1 pound carrots, chopped
1 onion, chopped
2 Tablespoons oil
6 Cups water
1/2 teaspoon salt
1/3 Cup parsley, chopped finely

Saute the chopped onions and carrots for 5 minutes in a large pot. Add water and salt. Bring to a boil. Reduce heat, cover, and simmer for 20 more minutes. Puree mixture and reheat.

CREAM OF BROCCOLI SOUP (Serves 8)

1 pound broccoli, chopped
1/2 pound mushrooms, chopped
1 small onion, chopped
1 teaspoon tarragon
3 Cups milk or soy milk
salt and pepper to taste

Steam vegetables and onion together for 10 minutes. Blend in blender or food processor half of the steamed vegetables and 1 1/2 Cups milk. Pour into a pot. Blend remaining vegetables and milk. Add to pot. Season and reheat for 5 minutes over medium heat. Add water if thinner soup is desired.

ZUCCHINI/POTATO CREAM SOUP (Serves 6)

1 small onion, chopped
2 Tablespoons oil
3 or 4 medium zucchini, chopped
2 potatoes, cubed in small pieces
6 Cups water
1/2 Cup rolled oats
1/2 teaspoon salt
2 Tablespoons parsley

Saute onion in oil. Add chopped zucchini and cubed potatoes. Saute for 5 minutes. Add water, oatmeal and seasoning. Simmer 15 minutes. Puree in blender, reheat, and serve.

Lunch Ideas

SPINACH/MUSHROOM SANDWICH
(Serves 6)

1 box frozen spinach
1 Cup mushrooms, sliced finely
1 pint sour cream
slices of bread or English muffins

Cook spinach and drain. Place cooked spinach and sliced mushrooms on bread. Cover with sour cream. Place in toaster oven under low heat until hot.

MOCK DANISH PASTRY (Serves 1)

2 Tablespoons water
1 apple, cored and sliced finely
dash of nutmeg or cinnamon
1 Tablespoon cottage cheese or crumbled tofu
1 slice whole wheat bread

Cook apple and nutmeg in water until sauce consistency is reached. Toast whole wheat bread. Spread with cottage cheese. Top with apple mixture. Place under broiler for five minutes.

Variation: Use applesauce or other cooked fruit.

POTATO PANCAKES (Serves 6)

3 Cups potatoes, mashed (precooked or canned)
1 onion, chopped
salt and pepper to taste
handful of parsley (optional)
3 Tablespoons oil

Add onion and seasonings to mashed potatoes. Fry in oiled pan until done on both sides.

RICE BURGERS (Serves 4)

2 Cups rice, cooked (instant rice or leftover rice)
1/2 Cup bread crumbs
1 Cup mixed vegetables, finely chopped (celery, carrots,
  squash, broccoli, etc.)
1/3 Cup oil
salt and pepper to taste

Mix rice, vegetables, seasonings, and bread crumbs
together. Form into patties. Brown in oiled frying pan
for 5-10 minutes on each side.

Variations: Add 1 or 2 eggs. Instead of rice, use barley.
Add onions.

MOCK "TUNA" SALAD (Serves 3)

1 Cup garbanzo beans (canned or pre-cooked)
1 stalk celery, chopped
1/2 small onion, minced finely
mayonnaise
salt and pepper to taste

Mash the garbanzo beans (chickpeas). Add remaining
ingredients and mix well. Spread on bread as a sandwich or serve on lettuce.

CORN FRITTERS (Serves 6)

2 Cups corn (fresh, frozen or canned)
1 Cup flour
1 1/2 Tablespoons corn starch
1 to 1 1/4 Cups water

Mix all ingredients in a bowl. Fry over medium heat in
oiled pan for 3-5 minutes, turning once.

Variations: Instead of corn use other vegetables.

QUICK PIZZA (Serves 6)

English muffins or whole wheat bread
1 Cup tomato sauce
slices of cheese
Italian seasoning
1/2 Cup topping (sliced onions, chopped green peppers,
   sliced mushrooms and/or sliced olives)

Toast English muffins. Spoon sauce over top of muffin.
Lay slices of cheese on top. Season. Put on optional
toppings. Put in broiler until cheese melts (approximately 5-10 minutes).

LENTIL BURGERS (Serves 6)

1 Cup lentils, pre-cooked in 2 1/2 Cups water
1 small onion, chopped finely
1/2 Cup wheat germ
1 teaspoon garlic salt
pepper to taste

Mix all the ingredients together and form six patties.
Fry on both sides in a pre-heated oiled pan over
medium heat. Garnish with lettuce and tomato and
serve on a roll.

Side Dishes

CAULIFLOWER AU GRATIN (Serves 4)

1 box frozen cauliflower
bread crumbs
strips of cheese
salt and pepper to taste
2 Tablespoons oil

Cook cauliflower and drain. Roll in bread crumbs. Place in oiled baking dish. Add strips of cheese. Bake at 350 degrees until cheese melts.

SCALLOPED CORN AND TOMATOES (Serves 6)

2 Tablespoons oil
4 tomatoes, sliced thickly
1 large can of corn (or box of frozen corn)
1/4 Cup margarine
1 Cup bread crumbs

Spread tomatoes on bottom of an oiled baking dish and mix the corn in. Top with bread crumbs and dot with margarine. Bake in oven at 350 degrees about 20 minutes until crumbs are toasted.

LEFTOVER POTATO DISH (Serves 6)

2 Cups leftover baked or boiled potatoes, sliced
1 onion, chopped
1 Cup leftover cooked vegetables
1/4 Cup oil
paprika, garlic salt and pepper to taste

In large oiled frying pan fry potatoes and onions. Add vegetables and seasoning. Heat 5 minutes.

GREEN BEANS WITH HERB SAUCE
(Serves 6-8)

2 boxes frozen French-style green beans
1 small onion, minced
1/4 Cup margarine
2 Tablespoons minced parsley
1/2 teaspoon thyme
3 Tablespoons lemon juice
salt and pepper to taste
1/4 teaspoon paprika

Cook green beans per directions on box. Drain and place in a serving dish. Saute onion lightly in margarine, add remaining ingredients and mix well. Heat gently and pour over beans.

SAUTEED MUSHROOMS (Serves 4)

1 pound mushrooms, chopped
1 large onion, chopped finely
3 Tablespoons margarine or oil
Seasonings - garlic powder, salt, pepper, etc.

In margarine saute mushrooms and onions. Season to taste. Cook over low heat for about 5-10 minutes until mushrooms are tender.

CABBAGE DISH (Serves 6-8)

1 head of cabbage, shredded
strips of American or Muenster cheese
1/2 Cup sesame seeds (optional)

Saute cabbage and seeds in oil until soft. Add strips of cheese and cook over low heat until cheese melts.

Variation: use lettuce, spinach, or bok choy instead of cabbage.

SPANISH RICE (Serves 3)

1 1/2 Cups rice, cooked (instant or leftover rice)
2 Tablespoons oil
1 onion, chopped finely
1 green pepper, chopped finely
1 small can tomato sauce
3 tomatoes, cubed
pepper, cumin, and chili powder to taste

In oiled frying pan saute onion and green pepper. Add cooked rice, tomatoes, tomato sauce and seasonings. Cook 10 more minutes.

SIMPLE STUFFED MUSHROOMS (Serves 4)

12 large mushrooms
1 small ripe avocado
1 ripe tomato, diced finely
pinch of cayenne pepper and garlic powder
salt to taste

Remove stems from mushrooms. Saute mushrooms for a few minutes until soft. Remove from heat and let cool. Mash avocado. Add tomato and spices. Mix well. Stuff mushrooms and serve.

FRIED ZUCCHINI AND SAUCE (Serves 4)

2 Tablespoons oil
2 pounds zucchini, sliced lengthwise 1/2" thick
Italian seasoning, salt and pepper to taste
8 ounces tomato sauce

In covered pan fry zucchini slices in oil with seasoning for 5 minutes over medium heat. Flip zucchini over, cover with sauce and continue cooking over low heat for 8-10 minutes. Serve. Sprinkle with cheese if desired.

SWEET AND SOUR CABBAGE (Serves 6)

1 small head cabbage, shredded (red and/or green)
1 apple, grated
1 onion, chopped
1/2 Cup raisins
2 Tablespoons oil
1 Cup water
2 Tablespoons flour
2 Tablespoons vinegar
1 Tablespoon brown sugar
1 Tablespoon salt

Saute onions and cabbage in oil. Add raisins, apples and 1/2 Cup water. Cook five minutes. In small jar shake up flour, vinegar, sugar, salt and 1/2 Cup water. Add to above and cook another 5 to 10 minutes.

Variation: Use pineapple instead of apples.

PASTA DISH (Serves 4)

1 pound of pasta, cooked and drained
1/4 Cup margarine
1/4 teaspoon each oregano, sweet basil and pepper
1/2 teaspoon garlic salt
3 Tablespoons Parmesan cheese or nutritional yeast
1/4 Cup chopped parsley (optional)

Melt margarine in a pan and add herbs. Stir in cooked pasta, sprinkle on cheese or yeast and serve.

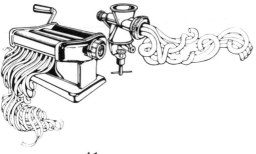

Main Dishes

RIGATONI COMBINATION (Serves 6)

1/3 pound rigatoni shells, macaroni or other pasta
1 onion, chopped
1 clove garlic, minced
1/2 green pepper, chopped
olive or vegetable oil
1 small can tomato sauce
1 pound can kidney beans, drained
1 teaspoon soy sauce or tamari
1/2 teaspoon chili powder
pepper and salt to taste

Cook pasta according to package directions. Saute onions, garlic, and green pepper 4-5 minutes or until soft. Stir in tomato sauce, kidney beans, soy sauce, salt, chili powder, and a shake of black pepper. Simmer several minutes to heat through. Drain pasta when done and stir into sauce. Serve as is or add 1/2 Cup cottage cheese to each serving to make a lasagna-like dish. Add hot sauce if desired.

TOMATO/EGGPLANT BAKE (Serves 4)

2 Tablespoons oil
1 small eggplant, peeled and cut into small pieces
1 can stewed tomatoes
1 onion, chopped finely
1 green pepper, chopped finely

Place eggplant, tomatoes, onion and green pepper in oiled baking dish. Cover with cheddar cheese if desired. Bake at 350 degrees until done (approximately 20 minutes).

BROCCOLI/KASHA BAKE (Serves 6)

1 box frozen broccoli
1 1/2 Cups kasha (often found in ethnic or gourmet
  sections of supermarkets)
slices of cheese
2 Tablespoons oil

Cook broccoli and drain. Cook kasha. Mash broccoli
and mix with kasha. Place in oiled baking dish. Cover
with strips of cheese. Bake at 350 degrees until cheese
melts.

LENTIL STEW (Serves 6)

1 Cup lentils
1 Cup macaroni
1 large can tomato sauce
1 small can tomato paste
1 onion, chopped
1 teaspoon Italian seasoning
1 teaspoon garlic powder or garlic salt
4 Cups water

Cook all ingredients in large pot until tender (approximately 20 minutes).

ZUCCHINI MOZZARELLA BAKE (Serves 4)

2 large zucchini, sliced
several slices of Mozzarella cheese
1 large can tomato sauce
salt and pepper to taste

Place alternating layers of the zucchini, Mozzarella
cheese, and tomato sauce in baking dish. Bake at 325
degrees for 20-25 minutes. Serve hot.

VEGETARIAN STEW (Serves 4)

1/2 Cup corn (fresh, frozen or canned)
1/2 Cup lima beans (frozen or canned)
1/2 Cup potatoes (precooked or canned)
1/2 Cup stewed tomatoes
1 onion, chopped
1 teaspoon oregano
1/4 Cup parsley, chopped
salt and pepper to taste

Mix above in large pot. Cook over low heat until hot (about 10-15 minutes). Serve alone or on rice.

LEFTOVER STEW (Serves 4)

1/4 Cup oil
1 small onion, chopped
1 green pepper, diced
3 stalks celery, diced
1/2 pound canned tomatoes
1 Cup leftovers (beans, legumes, seeds or nuts, raisins, grains, vegetables, olives, etc.)
salt, pepper and Italian seasoning to taste

Saute onion, green pepper and celery in oil. Add tomatoes, leftovers and seasonings. Cook over medium heat 10-15 minutes and serve.

MACARONI/CABBAGE DISH (Serves 4)

1/2 head cabbage, shredded
1 1/2 Cups macaroni, cooked
1 onion and green pepper, chopped
1/4 cup oil

In oiled pan saute cabbage, onion and green pepper. Add cooked macaroni and season with salt and pepper to taste. Serve hot.

VEGETABLE POT PIE (Serves 8)

Crust: (In a rush use store-bought pie crust.) This is a quick crust that can be used in many different recipes. White flour is OK also.

2 Cups whole wheat flour
1 teaspoon salt
1/2 Cup margarine
1/2 Cup water

Mix flour and salt in bowl. Work in margarine with fingers. Add water, stirring as little as possible to form a ball. Divide into 2 balls and roll out to 1/8" thickness. Prick pie shells and bake in a pie pan at 400 degrees for 10 minutes.

Vegetable Filling:

1/4 Cup oil
1 Cup onions, chopped
1 Cup celery, diced
1/2 Cup carrots, diced
1 1/4 Cups peas (fresh or frozen)

Saute above ingredients in oil until onions are soft.

In a separate bowl mix the following:

1/3 Cup oil
1/2 Cup flour
1 1/2 Cups water
1/2 teaspoon garlic powder
1 teaspoon salt
1/8 teaspoon pepper

Add above mixture to the sauteed vegetables. Pour into one pie shell and cover with the other. Bake at 350 degrees until crust is brown (approximately 15-20 minutes).

VEGETARIAN CHILI (Serves 6)

1/4 Cup oil
1 large onion, chopped
3 cloves garlic, minced
1 large green pepper, diced
3 Cups water
1 Cup kidney beans (precooked or canned)
4 tomatoes, cubed
1 Cup corn (fresh, frozen or canned)
1 teaspoon salt
1 teaspoon chili powder
pepper to taste

In large pot saute in oil the onion, garlic and green pepper until the onion is soft. Add water, kidney beans, tomatoes, corn, salt, chili powder, and pepper. Cook 25 minutes.

Variations: Add hot peppers, other vegetables such as carrots and celery, or add 2/3 Cup bulghur (cracked wheat). Pinto beans may be used instead of kidney beans.

RATATOUILLE (Serves 4)

1/4 Cup oil
3 tomatoes, cubed
1 large zucchini, diced
1 small eggplant, cubed
1 large green pepper, diced
1 large onion, chopped
2-3 cloves garlic, minced

In large frying pan saute in oil the tomatoes, zucchini, eggplant, peppers, onions and garlic. Cook over low heat for 10-20 minutes. Serve over rice or bread.

SPAGHETTI AND VEGETABLE SAUCE
(Serves 4)

Cook 1 pound of spaghetti and drain.

Sauce:

2 Tablespoons oil
1 onion, chopped
2 cloves garlic, minced
1 fifteen-ounce can tomato sauce
1 six-ounce can tomato paste
1 small zucchini, sliced
2 carrots, diced
1 Cup mushrooms, sliced
Italian seasoning, salt and pepper to taste

Saute onions and garlic in oil. Add sauce, paste, vegetables, and seasoning. Cook 20 minutes over low heat. Serve hot over cooked pasta.

FRIED EGGPLANT (Serves 4)

1 large eggplant, sliced
1/4 Cup oil
1 onion, chopped
3 cloves garlic, minced
1 Cup bread crumbs (or crushed corn flakes or matzo
  meal)

Slice eggplant. Add one Tablespoon oil to bread crumbs. Dip eggplant slices into crumbs. Fry eggplant in oil, onions and garlic.

Variation: Top with cheese, tomato sauce or Italian seasoning.

SPINACH PIE (Serves 8)

1 pre-made pie crust
2 1/2 Cups spinach (frozen or fresh)
1 1/2 Cups onions, chopped
3 cloves garlic, minced
1/3 cup oil
3 Cups Mozzarella cheese or tofu, crumbled
1 Tablespoon lemon juice
salt and pepper to taste

Cook spinach. Saute onions and garlic in oil. Add spinach, lemon juice, and cheese or tofu. Cook 5 minutes. Pour into pie crust. Bake at 350 degrees for 15-20 minutes until crust is brown.

Though tofu and tempeh are not common supermarket ingredients we have chosen to include them because they are very fast and convenient foods. We feel they may well be the yogurt of the 1990's. Even now, many supermarkets carry tofu.

Tofu and tempeh are both made from soy beans. If you've eaten in Chinese restaurants, you probably have eaten tofu. It would have been called soybean curd. Tofu is a bland food, but can be spiced up to make dips, desserts such as strawberry tofu cheesecake, and main dishes such as curried tofu or fried tofu to taste like chicken. Ask for tofu or bean curd in your nearby supermarket, or any Oriental specialty store.

Tempeh presently is much harder to find, but the search is well worth it. It has a meaty texture and can be prepared in a variety of ways. Tempeh can be purchased in most natural foods stores.

Soy Dishes

TOFU MAYONNAISE DIP (Serves 8)

16 ounces tofu, drained
1/2 teaspoon prepared mustard
2 teaspoons lemon juice
1/2 Cup olive or vegetable oil
1 large clove garlic, minced
1/2 teaspoon dill weed
1/4 teaspoon herb salt
1 Tablespoon soysauce or tamari
1/2 teaspoon hot sauce (optional)
1/2 teaspoon sweetener (optional)

Blend in blender or food processor until very smooth. Use as a dressing for potato, macaroni or rice salads, or as a dip for raw vegetables. If you want a plain type of mayonnaise, omit last four ingredients. (Don't use tabasco sauce, but rather Louisiana style hot sauce if you use hot sauce.)

FRIED TOFU (Serves 3-4)

1 pound tofu, drained and sliced
1 Cup flour (or nutritional yeast or wheat germ)
1/4 Cup soy sauce or tamari
2 Tablespoons oil
salt and pepper to taste

Slice tofu. Dip in soy sauce, then in flour. Season well with salt and pepper, then fry in oil over medium heat until brown (approximately 10 minutes).

FRIED TEMPEH SANDWICHES (Serves 3)

1 package tempeh (8 ounces)
3 Tablespoons oil
1 onion, chopped
salt and pepper to taste

Fry tempeh in oil with onions, approximately 5-10 minutes. Use in sandwiches. It can also be put in pita bread and served with tomatoes, cucumbers, mayonnaise or mustard with sprouts or lettuce.

SPAGHETTI AND TEMPEH SAUCE (Serves 4)

Cook 1 pound of spaghetti in a separate pot. Drain.

Sauce:
8 ounces tomato sauce
1 package tempeh (8 ounces)
1/2 teaspoon oregano
garlic salt to taste
3 Tablespoons oil
1 onion, chopped finely (optional)

Chop tempeh into small cubes. Saute in oil in a heated frying pan with seasoning. Add chopped onion, if desired, and tomato sauce. Heat 5 more minutes and serve over cooked spaghetti.

TOFU "EGGLESS" SALAD (Serves 6)

In a bowl mix the following ingredients well and serve alone or on toast with lettuce or sprouts.

1 pound tofu, crumbled
1 stalk of celery and one carrot, chopped finely
3 Tablespoons sweet relish
mayonnaise, pepper, salt and dill weed to taste

TOFU PIE AND QUICK CRUST (Serves 8)

Pie Crust: Blend 2 Cups granola and 1/4 Cup margarine together. Press into pie pan and bake for 10 minutes at 350 degrees.

Pie Filling: Blend together in a blender or food processor 1 pound of tofu, 3 Tablespoons carob fudge topping or chocolate syrup, 2 Tablespoons oil, 1 teaspoon vanilla and 4 dates that have been softened by soaking in a little boiling water for a few minutes. Blend until creamy, adding a little water if necessary.

Pour filling into pie crust and bake for 20 minutes. Serve chilled.

Variations: Instead of carob or chocolate syrup use fresh fruit such as chopped strawberries.

TOFU BURGERS (Serves 2)

1 Cup tofu, crumbled
1 teaspoon garlic powder
1/2 Cup wheat germ
1 teaspoon onion powder
1 Tablespoon soy sauce or tamari
1/2 teaspoon pepper
1/4 Cup parsley, chopped finely
1/4 Cup celery, chopped
1/4 Cup oil

Blend or mash tofu and add remaining ingredients. (The easiest way to do this is in a food processor, but you can do it by hand.) Mix well. Form patties and fry in a little oil on both sides.

Variation: Bake burgers instead of frying by first rolling patties in wheat germ. Lay in pan. Bake at 350 degrees until warm and light brown.

SUMMER TOFU SALAD (Serves 4)

1 pound tofu, cut in finger-size pieces
1 stalk celery, diced
2 scallions, chopped
1 large white radish, chopped
handful of parsley
1 very ripe tomato, chopped
1 Tablespoon tamari or soy sauce
1 teaspoon oil
pepper and salt to taste
lettuce leaves

Arrange pieces of tofu around perimeter of plate leaving empty circle in the middle. Sprinkle with celery, scallions, radish and parsley. Put tomato in center. Drizzle all over with tamari or soy sauce and oil. Season. Serve on lettuce.

Hint: This salad tastes better if it sits a while before serving.

CURRIED TOFU WITH PEANUTS (Serves 4)

3/4 Cup peanuts, whole or chopped
1 pound tofu, drained and cubed
3 Tablespoons oil
1 onion, chopped
1 teaspoon salt
2 cloves garlic, minced
1 teaspoon curry powder
1 Cup peas (fresh, frozen or canned)
1 carrot, diced

Saute onions and garlic in oiled frying pan. Add remaining ingredients and cook over medium heat for 10-20 minutes. Add a little water if needed.

Variations: Use garlic powder or ginger instead of garlic. Use different nuts and vegetables.

TOFU SPINACH DIP (Serves 8)

1/2 pound tofu
3 Tablespoons mustard or mayonnaise
10 ounce box frozen spinach (or fresh), cooked
1 large onion, chopped
2 cloves garlic, minced
2 Tablespoons oil
dash of pepper and tamari to taste

Saute onions and garlic in oil. Pour into blender, add remaining ingredients, and blend well. Serve with crackers or raw vegetables.

Chinese Cuisine

CHINESE MIXED VEGETABLES AND TOFU (Serves 6)

1/3 Cup oil
2 Cups vegetables, chopped (celery, carrots, green peppers, corn, bok choy, beans, pea pods, etc.)
8 ounces tofu, drained and cubed
soy sauce or tamari to taste

Stir fry ingredients in oil for 10-20 minutes. Serve alone or over rice.

STIR FRIED VEGETABLES, GINGER AND RICE
(Serves 6)

1/4 Cup oil
3 Cups mixed vegetables, chopped
1 1/2 Cups instant or leftover rice (precooked)
2 Tablespoons soy sauce or tamari
Ginger to taste, grated (about 1/4 teaspoon)

Saute vegetables in oil until soft. Add rice, soy sauce, and ginger to vegetables. Cook 10 more minutes.

FRIED RICE WITH PEANUTS OR ALMONDS
(Serves 6)

2 Cups instant rice or leftover rice (precooked)
1 Tablespoon oil
1 onion, chopped
1 green pepper, chopped
1 stalk celery, diced
1 Cup mushrooms, sliced
1 small zucchini, diced
3 Tablespoons soy sauce or tamari to taste
1 Cup peanuts or almonds, chopped or whole
2 eggs (optional), scrambled

Cut up vegetables. Saute onions in oil. Add all the other ingredients and stir fry for 15 minutes. Serve with Chinese noodles.

VEGETABLE CHOW MEIN (Serves 6)

3 Cups cooked rice (instant or leftover rice)
1/3 Cup oil
1 Cup bean sprouts (fresh or canned)
1 stalk celery, diced
1 green pepper, chopped
1 carrot, diced
2 tomatoes, cubed
soy sauce or tamari to taste
chow mein noodles (optional)

Saute in oil all the ingredients above for 10-20 minutes.
Serve with chow mein noodles.

MOCK FOO YOUNG (Serves 2)

10 ounces tofu, crumbled
salt and pepper to taste
1/4 teaspoon oregano
4 Tablespoons corn meal
1 carrot, grated
1 Tablespoon sesame seeds (optional)

Blend all ingredients well in a blender. Form four patties and fry in a little oil on both sides until light brown.

Variation: For a totally different taste cover patties with tomato sauce and sprinkle with cheese.

Mexican Fiesta

MEXICAN SUCCOTASH (Serves 6)

1/4 Cup oil
1 pound zucchini, sliced
1/2 Cup onions, chopped
1 green pepper, diced
1/4 Cup pimientos, diced
2 large tomatoes, chopped
1 1/2 Cups corn (frozen, fresh, or canned)
salt and pepper to taste

Saute onion in oil. Add remaining ingredients and simmer until vegetables are tender. Add a little water if necessary.

REFRIED BEANS (Serves 8)

3 Cups cooked pinto or kidney beans (canned or pre-cooked)
1 large onion, chopped
3 Tablespoons oil
9 ounces tomato paste
3-4 Tablespoons chili powder

Drain and mash cooked beans in a bowl. Saute onion in oil. Add tomato paste, chili powder and mashed beans. Cook over medium heat until beans are heated through.

Serve on chips or in taco shells with shredded lettuce, chopped tomatoes, hot sauce, olives, etc.

EASY TOSTADAS (Serves 6-8)

1 package Old El Paso enchilada shells (or substitute taco shells)
2 one-pound cans vegetarian chili
1 Cup shredded lettuce
1 cucumber, peeled and chopped
1 onion, chopped
1/2 Cup shredded cheese (optional)
Taco sauce to taste

Heat chili in pan. Lay shells in a single layer on a cookie sheet. Spread chili on each. Heat in a 400-degree oven for 5 minutes. Remove and let each person garnish with remaining ingredients as desired.

Note: This tastes good cold. Just put chili on tostada and garnish. Good for an emergency when traveling.

GUACAMOLE (Serves 4)

1 large or 2 small ripe avocados
1 small ripe tomato, chopped finely
garlic powder and cayenne pepper to taste

Mash avocados in a bowl. Add chopped tomato and seasoning. Mix well and serve on tacos, with chips or as a dip with raw vegetables.

Spreads And Dips

Spreads can be used for parties, snacks or light dinners. They not only taste good, but can be nutritious. But like many foods, if you eat too much, the calories will add up. Serve with crackers, breads, or raw vegetables such as carrots, celery, peppers, cauliflower, or zucchini.

ONION CHEESE DIP (Serves 6-8)

1 small onion, minced finely
2 Tablespoons oil
8 ounces cheddar cheese
3 Tablespoons mayonnaise
1/3 Cup water

Saute onions in oil. Pour into blender and add other ingredients. Blend well until smooth.

GARBANZO PEANUT SPREAD (Serves 8-10)

2 Cups garbanzo beans or chickpeas (canned or pre-cooked)
3 Tablespoons peanut butter
1/3 Cup lemon juice
1/8 teaspoon cumin
1/2 teaspoon garlic salt
pepper to taste
1/2 Cup water or as needed
1/4 Cup oil

Blend all the ingredients in a food processor or blender.

Variation: Instead of peanut butter use sesame butter (tahini) and add sauteed onions and parsley.

SPLIT PEA SPREAD (Serves 6-8)

3 1/4 Cups water
1 Cup split peas
1 carrot, diced finely
2 stalks celery, diced finely
1 small onion, chopped
1 teaspoon celery seed
salt and pepper to taste

Bring split peas to a rapid boil in water. Add carrots and celery. Then add onions and spices. Boil 15 minutes. Remove from heat and blend until smooth. Refrigerate until cool and serve.

NUT CHEESE (Serves 6)

1/2 Cup raw cashews
1/2 Cup water
4 Tablespoons lemon juice
3 Tablespoons oil
garlic powder and paprika to taste
1/2 small tomato, chopped

Blend cashews, water and lemon juice together. Slowly add oil. Then add remaining ingredients and blend well. Refrigerate before serving.

CREAM CHEESE OLIVE SPREAD (Serves 6)

8 ounces cream cheese
1 Cup olives, sliced
3 Tablespoons mayonnaise

Blend all ingredients well until smooth.

Variation: Add pickles.

BEWARE: This is extremely high in fat and salt!

COTTAGE CHEESE DIP FOR VEGETABLES
(Serves 8-10)

1 1/3 Cups low-fat cottage cheese or crumbled soft tofu
2 scallions, sliced
small clove garlic, minced
1 stalk celery, chopped
1/4 Cup fresh parsley leaves
1/4 teaspoon dried basil
1 teaspoon (or more) soy sauce or tamari
1/8 teaspoon Louisiana hot sauce
salt and pepper to taste

Combine all ingredients in blender and serve.

LENTIL PATE' (Serves 6-8)

1 Cup lentils, cooked in 2 Cups of water
1 onion, chopped
4 cloves garlic, minced finely
6 teaspoons margarine
1 teaspoon black pepper
1/2 teaspoon vinegar
water if necessary

Cook lentils. At the same time saute onions and garlic in margarine in a separate pan. Add pepper. Mix lentils, onions, garlic and pepper together. Blend in food processor or blender, adding water if necessary. Add vinegar last.

CHOPPED "LIVER" SPREAD (Serves 6)

3 Tablespoons oil
1/2 pound mushrooms, chopped
1 small onion, chopped
1 Cup chopped walnuts
salt and pepper to taste
1 Tablespoon water

Saute mushrooms and onion for 8 minutes. Pour into blender or food processor, adding walnuts, seasoning, and 1 Tablespoon water. Blend until smooth. Serve with matzo as a spread.

Desserts

SPICY DATE NUT SPREAD (Serves 4)

1/4 pound of dates, pitted
1/2 Cup hot water
1/2 Cup walnuts, chopped
1 apple, chopped
1/4 teaspoon cinnamon
pinch of ginger (optional)

Soak dates in hot water for a few minutes. Put mixture in blender, adding apple, nuts and spices. Blend until smooth.

COCONUT CLUSTERS (Serves 8)

2 Cups shredded coconut
4 ripe bananas, mashed
4 Tablespoons cocoa or carob powder
1 Cup walnuts, chopped

Blend ingredients together. Form clusters on a lightly oiled cookie sheet. Bake at 350 degrees for 20 minutes. Cool and remove from cookie sheet.

Variation: Instead of carob or cocoa powder use chopped fresh fruit such as strawberries.

OATMEAL COOKIES (Serves 8)

1 Cup margarine
1/2 Cup molasses or maple syrup
2 bananas
1/2 Cup water
1 3/4 Cups whole wheat flour
1 teaspoon baking soda
1 teaspoon baking powder
1 teaspoon cinnamon
1 teaspoon nutmeg
3 Cups rolled oats
1/2 cup raisins or chopped dates

Cream together margarine, bananas and molasses or syrup. Add remaining ingredients. Mix well. Drop a spoonful of batter at a time on an oiled cookie sheet. Bake 8 minutes at 400 degrees.

Variations: Add chopped walnuts to batter or chopped apples.

FRESH FRUIT SALAD AND PEANUT CREME (Serves 6-8)

Prepare fruit salad using your favorite fruits in season or if in a rush use canned fruit salad.

Peanut Creme:
1 Cup water
2 apples
1 Cup peanuts

Blend apples in 1/2 Cup water. Slowly add peanuts and remaining water as needed. Blend until smooth. Serve over fruit salad or baked apples and pears. Experiment with other types of nuts.

RICE PUDDING (Serves 6)

Cook 1 Cup instant rice as per directions, adding 2/3 Cup of raisins while cooking rice. Pour into blender, and add the following:

2 ripe bananas, peeled and mashed
1/2 Cup water
1 teaspoon cinnamon
1/4 teaspoon nutmeg

Blend together for 1 minute. Pour into glass baking dish. Bake for 20 minutes at 350 degrees.

Seasonal Party Ideas
For Twelve People

SUMMERTIME MENU:

Fruit salad
Bagels and/or rolls with cream cheese olive spread
Raw vegetable platter
Guacamole dip or cottage cheese dip
Assortment of nuts and seeds
Variety of dried fruit
Fruit juices and blended fruit drinks
Hot steamed corn

FRUIT SALAD (serves 12)

1/2 ripe watermelon, cut lengthwise
10 peaches, quartered
1 pint strawberries, sliced
1 pint blueberries
1 Cup raisins
1 Cup shredded coconut (optional)

Scoop out bite size pieces of watermelon and place in a large bowl. Add remaining ingredients. Mix well, and pour back into hollowed out watermelon. Keep chilled until serving.

2 DOZEN BAGELS OR ROLLS

1 POUND MARGARINE AND/OR CREAM CHEESE OLIVE SPREAD (cream cheese olive spread can sometimes be found in a supermarket, if not, use the recipe in this cookbook found on page 59)

RAW VEGETABLE PLATTER (Serves 12)

5 ripe tomatoes, sliced
1 pound carrots, sliced lengthwise into sticks
3 cucumbers, peeled and sliced
4 stalks celery, sliced lengthwise into sticks
1 pound olives
1 pound chopped broccoli or cauliflower
1 pound zucchini, sliced lengthwise into sticks

GUACAMOLE DIP OR COTTAGE CHEESE DIP
(see pages 57 and 60 in this cookbook for recipes)

2 POUNDS ASSORTED NUTS AND SEEDS

2 POUNDS ASSORTED DRIED FRUIT

2 GALLONS FRUIT JUICE (see page 26 to make blended fruit drink)

1 OR 1 1/2 DOZEN EARS OF CORN (steam indoors or outdoors over a barbecue, leaving the husk on if doing outdoors)

AUTUMN MENU:

Carrot cream soup
Ratatouille
Rice
Curried tofu with peanuts
Fresh apples
Apple cider or juice
Oatmeal cookies

CARROT CREAM SOUP (see recipe on page 33 of this cookbook and double the recipe)

RATATOUILLE (see recipe on page 46 of this cookbook and double the recipe)

RICE (either prepare 4 cups of plain instant rice, or prepare 2 Cups plain instant rice and 3 Cups Spanish rice using the recipe in this cookbook on page 40 and doubling the recipe)

CURRIED TOFU WITH PEANUTS (use the recipe in this cookbook on page 52 and double the recipe)

DOZEN FRESH APPLES (assorted colors if possible)

2 GALLONS APPLE CIDER AND/OR JUICE

OATMEAL COOKIES (use recipe in this cookbook on page 62 and double the recipe)

WINTERTIME MENU:

Vegetarian chili served on taco shells or with corn chips
Baked potatoes
Hot apple cider
Coconut clusters

VEGETARIAN CHILI (see recipe in this cookbook on page 46 and multiply the recipe by three)

24 TACO SHELLS

2 LARGE BAGS CORN CHIPS

SMALL HEAD OF LETTUCE, SHREDDED (serve on tacos)

1 POUND OF CHEESE, SHREDDED (serve on tacos)

2 ONIONS, CHOPPED FINELY (serve on tacos)

BOTTLE OF HOT SAUCE

12 BAKED POTATOES (serve with sour cream if desired or pour some chili over potato)

HOT APPLE CIDER (see recipe in this cookbook on page 26 and double the recipe)

COCONUT CLUSTERS (use recipe in this cookbook on page 62 and double recipe)

SPRING MENU:

Tofu "eggless" salad
Mock "tuna" salad
Cucumber salad
Breadsticks and onion cheese dip
Bread or rolls
Fresh fruit
Fruit juice

TOFU "EGGLESS" SALAD (see recipe in this cookbook on page 50 and double the recipe)

MOCK "TUNA" SALAD (see recipe in this cookbook on page 36 and double the recipe)

CUCUMBER SALAD (see recipe in this cookbook on page 29 and double the recipe)

2 BOXES BREADSTICKS

ONION CHEESE DIP (see recipe in this cookbook on page 58 and double the recipe)

2 LOAVES WHOLE WHEAT BREAD AND 1 1/2 DOZEN ROLLS

SIX TANGERINES, SIX ORANGES, BUNCH OF BANANAS, 2 BOXES OF STRAWBERRIES, A FEW APPLES

2 GALLONS ASSORTED FRUIT JUICES

If you are in doubt about your diet, you can use this plan prepared by Ruth Ransom, R.D. as a <u>GENERAL GUIDE</u>. Consult a dietitian or M.D. knowledgeable about nutrition if you have a special problem.

Meal Plan

A. PROTEIN FOODS: 1-2 SERVINGS PER DAY

1. one serving equals:

    1 1/2 Cups cooked dried beans or peas
    8 ounces tofu*
    4 ounces tempeh
    2 Cups fortified soy milk*
    1/2 Cup almonds*, cashews, walnuts, pecans
    1/4 Cup peanuts
    4 Tablespoons peanut butter
    2 Cups low-fat milk or yogurt*
    2 ounces cheese*
    1/2 Cup cottage cheese*
    2 eggs

B. WHOLE GRAINS: at least 6-8 SERVINGS/DAY

1. one serving equals:

    1 slice whole wheat, rye or whole grain bread
    1 buckwheat or whole wheat pancake or waffle
    1 two-inch piece cornbread
    2 Tablespoons wheat germ
    1 ounce wheat or oat bran
    1/4 Cup sunflower*, sesame*, or pumpkin seeds
    3/4 Cup wheat, bran or corn flakes
    1/2 Cup oatmeal or farina
    1/2 Cup cooked brown rice, barley, bulghur or corn
    1/2 Cup whole wheat noodles, macaroni or spaghetti

C. VEGETABLES: at least 4-6 SERVINGS/DAY

1. 2 or more servings/day of the following:

   1/2 Cup cooked or 1 Cup raw broccoli*, Brussel sprouts, collards*, kale*, chard*, spinach*, romaine, cabbage*, carrots, sweet potatoes, winter squash, tomatoes.

2. 2 or more servings/day (1 serving equals 1/2 Cup cooked or 1 Cup raw) of any other vegetable.

D. FRUITS: 4-6 SERVINGS/DAY

1. 2 servings/day of the following:

   3/4 Cup berries, 1/4 cantaloupe, 1 orange, 1/2 grapefruit, 1 lemon or lime, 1/2 papaya, 4-inch X 8-inch watermelon slice, or 1/2 Cup orange, grapefruit or vitamin C enriched juice.

2. 2-4 servings/day of other fruits:

   1 small piece fresh fruit
   3/4 Cup grapes
   1/2 Cup cooked fruit or canned fruit without sugar
   2 Tablespoons raisins, dates or dried fruit

E. FATS: 0-4 SERVINGS/DAY

1. 1 serving equals:

   1 teaspoon margarine, butter or oil
   2 teaspoons mayonnaise or salad dressing
   1 Tablespoon cream cheese, gravy or cream sauce

F. STARRED(*) FOOD ITEMS: 2, 3 OR MORE SERVINGS/DAY

1. Men include 2 choices daily
2. Women include 3 choices each day

G. EXCEPTIONS:

1. Pregnant women, persons under 18 and persons with bone or muscle trauma or other special needs may require additional servings.

2. Vegans (vegetarians that also don't use dairy products and eggs) need to include a vitamin B-12 source weekly. Sources include: some brands of nutritional or primary yeast, and vitamin enriched or fortified foods such as Grape-Nuts cereal and Pillsbury's Green Giant Harvest Burgers.

SAMPLE TWO DAY MENU

	BREAKFAST	LUNCH	DINNER	SNACKS
DAY 1	French Toast orange juice	split pea soup biscuits celery with cream cheese fresh fruit	tomato eggplant bake macaroni, peas and corn pear halves	graham cracker milk
DAY 2	bran, corn or wheat flakes and milk banana	peanut butter and sliced apples on whole wheat bread carrot/raisin salad	cheese omelet with vegetables wheat toast steamed broccoli baked potato	ginger snaps lemon- ade

Vegetarianism On The Job

A common problem vegetarians encounter is finding something to eat while working. Cafeterias often offer very little food that we can consume besides salads or perhaps yogurt. As a result, vegetarians must often bring their own lunch. What happens when you have to attend a business luncheon or travel? The following are true stories written by those in the working world who have learned how to cope in a meat-eating society. We also include ideas for mothers or fathers whose job is to raise children.

A TEACHER

The first year I became a strict vegetarian (a vegan) I was director of an elementary school day care program located in the Virginia suburbs of Washington, D.C. As most people know, school lunch programs are nothing to brag about these days. Overall, the only things I could eat from the menu were the occasional carrot and celery sticks, raisins, prunes, an apple, banana or orange. This certainly wasn't a suitable meal, so I had to brown bag it everyday. This turned out to be a positive step.

Each day I'd bring in a new lunch. The initial comments I received from the five-year-olds ranged from "What's that?" and "That looks strange" to "How can you eat that?", and of course "Yuck!" These remarks referred to tofu dips, vegetable casseroles, tempeh sandwiches, and bulghur dishes.

Slowly the children began to ask questions about my eating habits. I explained to them that I was a vegetarian because I didn't like to eat animals. Often a good conversation evolved. Some children eventually were brave enough to ask for a taste of my lunch. Of course, I encouraged them. Usually, if the first child liked the dish, ten others would then want to try the "new" food.

This was all very exciting to me. Most of the children didn't enjoy the school meals. They'd end up going hungry rather than eating the food. I provided them with one snack a day, such as peanut butter and crackers, raisins, etc. The children were all happy with this.

I was lucky that at this job my co-workers usually supported my desire to give the children "healthy" snacks. The past few years, however, I have been teaching in various places including a junior high school, an adult education program, and a community college. Most of the teachers have been heavy meat eaters, smokers, coffee drinkers and junk food addicts. A few admire my eating style; others have no interest in learning about vegetarianism.

I now tend to eat in my own classroom instead of the cafeteria. When I have to attend luncheons or conferences I either tell them in advance that I am a vegetarian or else nibble on whatever vegetarian food I can find. Once I attended a meal served by the home economics department. A teacher remembered I was vegetarian and made sure there was something I could eat. No one commented about my dietary habits. The others simply ate their chicken and I ate a salad. In retrospect, I wish some of the instructors teaching nutrition had asked me some questions. Perhaps they would then have become more familiar with vegetarian diets and would be able to serve more than salads.

AN ELECTRICAL ENGINEER

Riding down Interstate 95, Mort, an electrical engineer told us his story.

Let me begin with what I bring to work. I always have several handfuls of nuts for snacks. On the weekend, I bake bread. My non-vegetarian roommate sometimes asks for tastes, so I'll bake an extra loaf to give to him. For lunch, I'll bring three slices of the homemade bread, some fruit, and herbal tea. New people will say "What is that bread you're eating?" I give them a taste, then they're normally impressed enough not to bug me.

Being a vegetarian sometimes makes it hard to be social. In this country, eating is always the way to get to know people. I'll go out to eat if there's something for me to order. Chinese restaurants and salad bars are good. I can always get a bean burrito in a Mexican restaurant. People are pretty understanding when I won't go out with them. Even waiters recognize I'm average. When I order a vegetable plate, they ask if I'm on a diet or a vegetarian.

Why did I become a vegetarian? It was a leg of lamb I was eating. I realized it looked just like part of me. I couldn't eat meat from then on. The transition wasn't difficult for me. I had a few friends who were vegetarian and they gave me a morale boost. I didn't feel any peer pressure. I guess I like to be different. People would say to me, "You have to be more careful when you eat."

"Don't you?" I'd respond. I would then ask them if they knew where they got different vitamins. They had no idea.

A SOCIAL WORKER

I work in a psychiatry outpatient service at a hospital. Most of the staff have lived sheltered naive lives and are limited in their eating habits. A few did try being vegetarian once, but gave up.

For lunch, I generally bring homemade yogurt, fruit, cheese sandwiches, and soup. People are curious and will say, "Tina's got her food." Even clients keep me in mind. They'll tell me I can eat with them today because the cafeteria's serving cheese sandwiches. Sometimes I'll share what I bring. Once the staff ate my rice crackers. They got very upset when they found out the crackers contained seaweed. I asked them how they could drink colas, etc. They couldn't even pronounce the ingredients in those foods. At least they know what seaweed is.

A lot of clients who never smoked before begin to smoke a lot in the hospital. They drink a lot of soda, coffee and sugar. Then they start gaining weight. I try to get some patients to eat wheat bread and not white. So I say something to them in moderation.

I gradually changed my own diet. In college, I cut out red meat for health reasons. I like the taste of chicken, but don't feel good about how they're raised. Also, I think chicken's greasy, even in soups. I grew up in upstate New York. We would often buy a whole pig and cut it up. But we also ate a lot of healthy foods like dandelion greens and lentils. I guess it may be my German background. Today my family is accepting my food habits. They've become much more aware of the issues surrounding vegetarianism.

COUNSELOR/ACTIVIST

In 1974 I was in a college business administration program. During a discussion with my roommate, I claimed to be against killing.

"You eat meat, don't you?" he responded.

"Yes," I nodded my head. I never thought about it before. Having grown up in a typical heavy meat-eating family, I often ate salami, bologna, and hamburgers for snacks instead of cookies. I never met a vegetarian and always thought of them as spaced out health freaks living on brown rice and sprouts. I asked my friend, "Do you know any vegetarians?"

"Ronald Boyle," he responded. "But he eats McDonalds' hamburgers. He says they're not really meat."

"Anyone else?" I pressed.

"Not really."

I thought about it for a day and the thought left me. Not killing animals made sense, but I couldn't do it. People eat meat.

Six months later, I had the privilege of traveling through Europe on a train pass. We were on the $10 a day budget plan, including lodging. I feasted on Spanish steak, Norwegian fish, and German salami. The last day of the trip, vegetarianism for the first time in six months popped back into my mind. I thought of the unnecessary killing. I just tried so many different foods, I didn't need to eat them again. "Wayne, I'm going to be a vegetarian," I announced.

From that day on I ate no meat, fish or chicken.

It never occurred to me that killing fish could be any different than killing any other animal. Perhaps, as my my brother reminds me, this is because of what happened in early fishing trips with my father and uncle. I was five or six. While other fishermen threw the aquatic creatures to the bottom of their rowboats, our unbroken rule was to place them in a bucket of water so they wouldn't suffer. Killing had to be instant.

The first test for my vegetarianism was Pizza Hut. I dined on pizza, salad and vegetable soup which had beef stock. I knew not to order soup again. That summer, working at the New Jersey shore, my diet consisted mostly of pizza, eggplant subs, omelettes and cottage cheese. My mom warned me against consuming too much cholesterol, but otherwise was supportive.

I searched for more information in libraries and health food stores, but to no avail. Anything close seemed too flaky and reminded me of starving Indians eating rice. Finally, I happened upon Nat Altman's Eating for Life. I am forever grateful to him for this balanced scientific approach.

Surprisingly, no one hassled me for my beliefs. Back at school I met a woman who had also recently turned vegetarian. Several others followed our lead and became transient vegies for health reasons. Most soon fell by the wayside. But the cafeteria was very kind in preparing special meals for us. For example, when they had lasagna, they'd prepare a dish without meat.

I was slow to find other vegetarians. For a year, even living in New York City, I came upon no one more knowledgeable than I. Then I hit upon a gold mine. In a newspaper, I read about a vegetarian group. One month later, a friend and I visited their rural estate nestled between several farms.

We were seated at a bridge table in the dining room. After ten minutes, a woman entered with two small bowls of orange pudding-like substance topped with coconut. She placed the dishes on the table and disappeared. We stared at the bowls for a minute with questioning looks and words. With no other signs of human life around, we were on our own. We dipped in a teaspoon, picking up about a milligram of the sticky substance. After touching the spoon to our tongue, we scooped up a bit more. "Not bad." We increased the sticky dosage to half a teaspoon. It was heavy, not at all like pudding. We continued exploring and dug down a little deeper into the bowls. We hit paydirt! Bananas. Yum. That was our reward for taking a chance on this mysterious foodstuff. Still having no idea what it was, we gobbled up the bananas so our bodies would be sure not to revolt.

Our hostess returned to pick up the empty bowls. I carefully asked her what the delicious treat was.

"Oh, it's blended apricots with tahini," she nonchalantly told us. "You've never had it before?" she asked in her quiet voice.

Today, vegetarianism is much less mysterious. But in eight years of working with vegetarian organizations, I still hear many of the same practical questions. People want to be vegetarian, but feel it's not for the average working person. I hope this book and stories from ordinary people will answer some of your doubts and questions.

AN ENGLISH WORKING MOTHER

Before the birth, I remember reading books by Grantly Dick Read on <u>Natural Child Birth</u> and going to relaxation clinics to learn how to relax during labor. I had raspberry leaf tea just before going to the hospital and Jackie was born six hours after! - a normal healthy six pound, two ounces, little girl. I thanked God for her safe delivery and a healthy baby. As I had done some midwifery before, I knew of a few helpful tips such as rubbing olive oil on my tummy to prevent stretch marks after the pregnancy.

The first six months were easy really, as I breast fed Jackie completely. I only put on fourteen pounds in weight while I carried her and had a good vegetarian menu throughout the pregnancy with plenty of fruit and vegetables and I had ample milk to feed her. I knew this was the right thing to do, being the most natural and hygienic food a baby needs, also the right temperature and cheapest.

I had been a vegetarian about two years then as I was having a battle against very painful rheumatoid arthritis that I had contracted at the age of twenty-one while a nurse. I had decided that becoming a vegetarian was one way I could get a more alkaline blood stream and help myself recover, and I decided that Jackie would benefit, too. I read extensively from different books- one being <u>On Having a Baby Easily</u> by Margaret Brady. She advocated a vegetarian lifestyle for healthy children. When Jackie was six months old, I remember sending away for "Holle" baby food- a cereal organically grown that I had seen advertised in a magazine, <u>Health for All</u>. Jackie liked this and I supplemented it with whole wheat musks, fresh fruit juices, mashed bananas, prunes and sieved vegetables. I had a "mouli" grater at that time which was a help and I used it to grate carrots finely and squeezed them in a sterilized cheese cloth to get pure carrot juice for her. There were no expensive blenders in those days which now make life easier. Jackie loved boiled eggs and St. Ivel lactic cream cheese. She had no meat, fish or so called "junk foods."

When it came to school at five years old, I packed her a lunch which she ate at school or in a nearby park. I often cycled there to meet her on my lunch break from work nearby. Then we would have our main meal in the evenings. This routine continued at her senior Folkestone girls' grammar school. You could have a cooked school dinner at the school canteen- but being a vegetarian she would not be specially catered for, so I always made whole wheat sandwiches with fruit or/and yogurt, nuts and raisins, etc. At a nearby Technical girls school where there were several vegetarian children and a very sympathetic deputy headmistress- a special menu was cooked for them and they sat at their own "vegie" table. I might add that this is not very usual at English schools, though we do have St. Christopher's which is a completely vegetarian boys school. They grow a lot of their own organic vegetables.

I really had no big problems. Jackie would go to parties as other children did, but never wanted meat. "I do not want to eat animals," she said as a child.

I wrote to Margaret Brady once for advice when Jackie had some tonsil trouble. She said to cut out milk and milk products for a week or so and do a little semi-fast, just juice and fruit for a day or two. This helped a lot. I was learning. Jackie only had about two days off from school for sickness during her school life, though she had measles before she started school. This says a lot for a vegetarian diet, I think.

A FINANCIAL ANALYST

I work for a large corporation in mid-town Manhattan where I manage a financial group. The environment in the finance department is very conservative, with stiff pressure to conform, in all ways, to a certain unwritten style, which includes hair, dress, hobbies and lifestyle in general. It is difficult to get along in the business world and not conform to certain standards. A total vegetarian diet is generally seen as being somewhat radical in a conservative environment, although I do know one other person in the financial department who is vegetarian.

At this point, I can see some work-related advantages to following a vegetarian diet. My diet is low in fat, so I have no trouble maintaining a normal weight. Corporate interest is moving in the direction of wellness, so vegetarian diets may even be looked upon more favorably for their inherent healthfulness than they were ten or fifteen years ago. My wife is a vegetarian nutritionist, so I think that increases my credibility a little and makes me look less "radical."

On the other hand, my choices are limited at lunchtime if I eat in the company cafeteria. Selection is improving, though, as more people are requesting "light" foods, low-fat foods, etc., for health and weight control reasons. When I travel by plane, my secretary automatically orders vegetarian meals for me.

One final note from a financially-oriented mind---vegetarian diets save money, both at the grocery store and in terms of investing in future good health!

RAISING A VEGETARIAN CHILD

Sarah is a fourteen-month old vegan baby who has thus far been blessed with superb health. I can't help but believe that her diet has had a positive influence on her health. Two of Sarah's non-vegetarian friends live in similar non-smoking environments, are female, are first born and are fourteen months old. Both girls have had numerous ear infections, colds and several bouts of intestinal virus. Sarah had an intestinal virus with diarrhea for thirty-six hours when she was four months old. Her nose runs when she's teething or if she's been exposed to excessive cigarette smoke. So she's not invulnerable. She's human too. I have often wondered what the "normal" state of health would be if all children were vegetarian and lived in a smoke-free environment.

If I compare Sarah with her cousins the difference is more striking. All five cousins, four males and one female, have had colds, ear infections, and high fever by the time they were one year old. Two had been hospitalized (pneumonia and staph infection of the stomach) before one year of age and one cousin missed his first birthday because of scarleting. Of the three families involved, all are omnivorous, one is non-smoking, and all consider themselves to be, "normal", healthy families.

I believe Sarah's strict vegan diet has made a positive difference in her health and in mine, too. I have been ill once in six years and it was a stomach virus. Many people succumbed, but it was a blow to my ego. The sickness lasted twenty-four hours. Perhaps my ego needed to learn a lesson. A vegetarian diet has not made me invulnerable to disease, but the rare time I fell ill, it did make a positive and noticeable difference in the severity and duration of the illness.

"What will I feed my child?" At first this question was particularly worrisome to me. Commercial baby food, for the most part, was unacceptable to me because it contained animal products, sugar or starch fillers. Even the plain vegetables (there are a few) and fruits seem overprocessed, dead and taste awful. So I started making my own baby foods. Here are some of my recipes.

7 GRAIN CEREAL WITH BANANAS

Cook cereal according to the directions on the package. Mix equal parts cereal and banana and grind in a baby food grinder. Mix only as much as the baby will eat. This recipe does not taste the same the second time it is served.

BROCCOLI WITH TOFU

Thinly slice broccoli and steam five to eight minutes and no more. Blend with 1/3 block of tofu.

APPLE PEAR DESSERT

Core and slice three apples and two pears. Cook in half to one cup apple juice or water. Add half cup raisins and cook until plump. Blend. This may be frozen.

FAMILIA

Familia is a commercial baby food cereal made of whole grains, chopped nuts, and dried fruits. It is not recommended until a baby is six months of age.

(Sarah's mother sings opera at the Kennedy Center in Washington, D.C.)

A GOVERNMENT WORKER

The Department of the Interior has its endangered species list, but there are many who feel it is okay to slaughter other creatures. Humans, animals, and for that matter all beings should be placed on the endangered species list.

People discriminate against animals. They will be so concerned about a pet or a few animals brought to their attention by the media, and yet condone the killing of the farmyard bird and other animals- especially those they eat.

Animals and the sick are slaves to mankind. The abolition of such slavery could cause an economic disaster.

It is hard for me to live in a world surrounded by meat eaters. I have to work and be governed by such persons who do not have the minuteness of compassion, respect or reverence for the right to life of all creatures on land, in the air and sea. I do not know if it's ignorance or meanness that makes people continue to eat meat once they've been well informed of the vegetarian philosophy.

A REGISTERED DIETITIAN

As a registered dietitian, I have worked in a variety of settings, from hospitals and nursing homes to a wellness center. I've been lacto-ovo vegetarian for eleven years. At one time I tried to keep a low profile as far as my eating habits are concerned, not wanting to draw attention to my "radical" ways. I found, though, that everyone seems to notice what nutritionists eat, so it wasn't so easy to hide.

With the focus today on fitness and good health, it's much easier to be a vegetarian nutritionist. Until only a few years ago, I was always eyed a little suspiciously by co-workers, but now I am seen as "practicing what I preach." I no longer try to hide my eating habits and, instead, am much more pointed in advice I give to clients. It's much easier to counsel people on the merits of vegetarianism now that medical literature and research is turning up new benefits of vegetarian diets every day. I can already see a marked increase of interest in vegetarian diets; I have more and more clients coming to me for counseling saying they want to try giving up meat. I think this will snowball because vegetarian diets are being linked now with everything from prevention of cancer to lower incidence of osteoporosis, and everything in between!

It's going to take some time for workplaces to catch up with the new interest in health and fitness. Employee cafeterias don't offer the greatest selections for lunches. I almost always bring my own food from home. Sometimes I'm the only one in the cafeteria with a brown bag. My tofu salad sandwiches and baked sweet potatoes generate a lot of questions and give me an opportunity to educate others.

Nutritional Information

SOURCES OF PROTEIN

Lentils, low-fat dairy products, seeds, peas, chickpeas; Many common foods such as potatoes, pizza, greens, and corn quickly add to your protein intake.

EGG REPLACERS

bananas - 1 for 1 egg

arrowroot flour - 2 TB for 1 egg

cornstarch - 2 TB for 1 egg

SOURCES OF B-12

fortified cereals (such as Grape-Nuts), some brands of nutritional yeast, analogs, and soy milk. Read labels.

SOURCES OF CALCIUM

low-fat milk and dairy products, kale, collards, broccoli, tofu, almonds, sunflower seeds...

VEGETARIAN FOODS HIGH IN FAT

cheeses, butter, avocado, oil, nuts, whole milk, coconut, margarine and eggs. VEGETABLES DO NOT CONTAIN CHOLESTEROL, but some may contain saturated fat.

SOURCES OF IRON

watermelon, lentils, collards, kale, oatmeal, broccoli, strawberries, split peas and chick peas.

On the following page is a sample list of nutrients in foods. You can find tables for common items in the U.S.D.A. Home and Garden Bulletin Number 72 Nutritive Values of Foods, available from the Superintendent of Documents, U.S. Government Printing Office, Washington, D.C. 20402. This is appropriate for most consumer uses. More extensive books are U.S. Department of Agriculture Handbook Number 8 or Agriculture Handbook Number 456, which are available from the Superintendent of Documents or your local library. Laurel's Kitchen also has very useful nutrition information.

The Recommended Daily Allowances (RDA) are the amounts of nutrients recommended by the Food and Nutrition Board, and are considered adequate for maintenance of good nutrition in healthy persons in the United States.

Please note that in an equal amount of calories, greens such as kale and collards have more calcium, iron, and protein than beef. One cup of skim cottage cheese would give you more protein than equal calories of beef. The key to a healthy vegetarian diet is to eat a wide variety of foods. If you were eating only meat and no vegetables, you would have a hard time meeting your dietary needs.

TURN PAGE FOR NUTRIENT CHART

Nutrient Chart

FOOD	AMOUNT	CALORIES	PROTEIN (g)	CALCIUM (mg)	IRON (mg)
cottage cheese					
2% low-fat	1 Cup	205	31	155	.4
large curd	1 Cup	235	28	135	.3
American cheese					
processed	1 oz.	95	6	163	.2
milk					
whole	1 Cup	150	8	291	.1
non-fat milk	1 Cup	85	8	302	.1
egg	large, raw no shell	80	6	28	1.0
beef ground (lean with 21% fat)	2.9 oz. patty	235	20	9	2.6
watermelon with rind and seeds	4" x 8" wedge	110	2	30	2.1

bread, whole wheat	1 slice	65	3	24	.8
Oatmeal	1 Cup	130	5	22	1.4
lentils, cooked	1 Cup	210	16	50	4.2
green beans, cooked, drained, frozen cut	1 Cup	35	2	54	.9
broccoli, cooked, drained from 1 Cup chopped, frozen	1 Cup	50	5	100	1.3
cabbage, raw, finely shredded	1 Cup	20	1	44	.4
collards, cooked, drained, from raw leaves without stems	1 Cup	65	7	357	1.5
kale, raw leaves cooked and drained	1 Cup	45	5	206	1.8
RDA female 25-50 non-pregnant, non-lactating		1900-2200	50	800	15
RDA male 25-50		2300-2900	63	800	10

Spices For
Vegetarian Cookery

Types and amounts of spices will vary according to your cooking style. Below are some combinations that have proved to work well. Experiment and enjoy!

ALLSPICE

cakes
breads
baked fruit
beverages

CELERY SEED

soups
coleslaw
potato salad
casseroles
mayonnaise

CHILI POWDER

stews
bean dishes

CINNAMON

oatmeal
breads
teas
apple dishes
cottage cheese
fruit dishes

CUMIN

Mexican dishes
spreads
chili

CURRY POWDER

Indian dishes
rice dishes
tofu
eggs
salads

GARLIC POWDER

Italian dishes
beans
salads
bread
vegetables
soups
dips and spreads

MARJORAM

stews
squash
egg dishes
soups

MINT

vegetables
ice cream
tea
tabbouli

NUTMEG

apple pie
cheese dishes
desserts

OREGANO

beans
pizza
Mexican dishes
tomato dishes
vegetables
Italian dishes
chili

PAPRIKA

hash browns
Deviled eggs
vegetables
salads
rice
casseroles
cottage cheese

PARSLEY

salads
bread stuffing
dips
soups
stews

ROSEMARY

dips and spreads
vegetables
soups

TARRAGON

green salads
tomato dishes

THYME

peas and carrots
cheese dishes
onion soup

True or False?

1. Vegetarians have to worry about combining proteins.

2. Milk is the only good source of calcium.

3. Vegetarians have to worry about B-12.

4. To be a vegetarian, I have to shop in a health food store and spend a lot of money.

5. Vegetarian cooking is complicated. I have to change my whole lifestyle to be a vegetarian.

6. Becoming a vegetarian will help me lose weight.

7. Animals in most food advertisements are smiling because they enjoy the good treatment given on small family farms.

ANSWERS:

1. FALSE Vegetarians easily meet their protein needs by eating a varied diet, as long as they consume enough calories to maintain their weight. It is not necessary to plan combinations of foods. A mixture of proteins throughout the day will provide enough essential amino acids. (See "Position of The American Dietetic Association: Vegetarian Diets," JADA, March 1988, and A Vegetarian Sourcebook by Keith Akers).

In using the concept of limiting amino acids, many people wrongly assumed this meant there was none of that amino acid in the food. In fact, most foods contain at least some of all essential amino acids. Exceptions are some fruits and empty calorie or junk foods.

Another important fact is that the body maintains a relatively constant supply of essential amino acids in what is called the amino acid pool. This pool is made up of amino acids from endogenous sources (digestive secretions and desquamated cells) with only a small portion from the diet. The ability of the body to recycle amino acids reassures us that essential amino acids do not need to be eaten in any specific pattern of mealtime or type of food.

Again, the points to remember are consume a variety of wholesome foods including some protein-rich vegetables and obtain sufficient calories.

2. FALSE One cup of whole milk has about 291 mg. of calcium. One cup of cooked collard greens has 357 mg. of calcium. One hundred grams of whole milk has about 118 mg. while one hundred grams of tofu (72 calories) has about 128 mg.

3. FALSE Most vegetarians eat eggs or dairy products which contain B-12. Vegetarians generally are able to meet their B-12 needs from these sources. Supplements are not necessary. If you do not consume eggs or milk, B-12 can easily be obtained from fortified foods such as some brands of nutritional yeast (Red Star T-6635+, etc.), which is not brewers yeast, Grape-Nuts cereal, Eden Soy Extra soy milk, and Pillsbury's Green Giant Harvest Burgers. Many other common foods also have B-12. As in any diet, it is helpful to read labels.

4. FALSE You can continue to shop at your local supermarket. If you stay away from processed foods and expensive cheeses, a vegetarian diet will probably be much cheaper than a meat diet. Compare the price of a salad bar to a steak dinner!

5. FALSE Like every other diet, vegetarianism can be complicated or simple. If you are eating eggs and milk, there are no special considerations for a vegetarian diet. You can continue to eat in the same restaurants and order foods such as eggplant parmesan, spaghetti, salad bars, French fries, fondues, egg salad sandwiches, and so on. An added bonus is that you will probably save money by ordering these dishes.

6. FALSE Again, a vegetarian diet is like any other diet. Fat has twice as many calories as carbohydrates and proteins. If you have a normal metabolism, and overconsume high-fat foods such as high-fat dairy products, peanut butter, avocados, or cook with too much oil, and do not burn up or eliminate these excess calories, you will probably gain weight no matter what the sources of these calories.

7. FALSE In our observations of animals before slaughter, we have not seen any smiling animals. In order to raise animals for food economically, the animals are kept in crowded conditions. Cows are penned up for several months before slaughter without being allowed to exercise. This prevents the meat from becoming tough. One chicken house could easily contain thousands of chickens, who have very short lives, and do not get to see outside sunlight. Factory farm animals usually are fed antibiotics to prevent illnesses.

Resources

Akers, Keith. A Vegetarian Sourcebook, Putnam, 1983

Dyer, Judith. Vegetarianism: An Annotated Bibliography, Scarecrow Press, 1982

Gandhi, Mahatma. Gandhi, An Autobiography, Beacon Press, 1971

"Position of The American Dietetic Association: Vegetarian Diets," Journal of The American Dietetic Association, Vol. 88:3, 1988

Robertson, Laurel. The New Laurel's Kitchen, Ten Speed Press, 1986

Schwartz, Richard. Judaism and Vegetarianism, Micah Publications, 1988

"Senate Select Committee on Nutrition Dietary Goals for the United States," November, 1977

Seventh Day Adventist Dietetic Association The Diet Manual, 1989. Includes vegetarian meal plans used by dietitians in hospitals.

Singer, Peter. Animal Liberation, Avon Books, 1975

United States Department of Agriculture, Nutritive Value of Foods, 1981

Beauty Without Cruelty, 175 W. 12th St., N.Y.C., N.Y. 10011 Lists alternatives to animal products.

Center for Science in the Public Interest, 1875 Connecticut Avenue N.W., Suite 300, Washington, D.C. 20009-5728. Write for their publications list. They publish a newsletter, full color nutrition posters, etc.

Jewish Vegetarians of North America, 6938 Reliance Road, Federalsburg, MD 21632 (410) 754-5550.

People for the Ethical Treatment of Animals (PETA), 501 Front Street, Norfolk, VA 23501 (757) 622-PETA. They promote activism and animal rights.

Physicians Committee for Responsible Medicine, P.O. Box 6322, Washington, D.C. 20015.

The Vegetarian Resource Group, P.O. Box 1463, Baltimore, MD. 21203 (410) 366-VEGE.

FOR MORE INFORMATION ABOUT VEGETARIANISM:

Publications by The Vegetarian Resource Group include: *Meatless Meals for Working People -- Quick and Easy Vegetarian Recipes* $6.00, *Simply Vegan - Quick Vegetarian Meals* $13.00, *Simple, Lowfat and Vegetarian* $15.00, *No-Cholesterol Passover Recipes* $9.00, and *The Lowfat Jewish Vegetarian Cookbook* $15.00. To join, order books, ask questions about vegetarian issues, or find out about local vegetarian groups in your area, write or send a check to The Vegetarian Resource Group, P.O. Box 1463, Baltimore, MD 21203.

Join The Vegetarian Resource Group and receive the bi-monthly 36-page *Vegetarian Journal*. This non-profit educational organization works on a local and national level to educate others about vegetarianism. Membership is $20 per year.

MEMBERSHIP APPLICATION

NAME _____

ADDRESS _____

_____ ZIP _____

TELEPHONE _____

Send $20 check to *The Vegetarian Resource Group*, PO Box 1463, Baltimore, MD 21203; charge your membership over the phone by calling (410) 366-8343; or e-mail us at TheVRG@aol.com All members receive the bi-monthly *Vegetarian Journal.*

Be sure to visit our World Wide Web Page at http://www.envirolink.org/arrs/VRG/home.html